D1488877

Michael Imperioli, Dino (the rooster), EJ Caroll, and Raul Aranas
in a scene from the Studio Dante production of *Chicken*.

CHICKEN

BY MIKE BATISTICK

★

★

DRAMATISTS
PLAY SERVICE
INC.

CHICKEN made its Off-Broadway premiere at Studio Dante (Michael and Victoria Imperioli, Artistic Directors) in New York City on February 28, 2007. It was directed by Nick Sandow; the set and costume design were by Victoria Imperioli; the lighting design was by Tony Giovannetti; the sound design was by David Margolin Lawson; the production stage manager was Justin Scribner; the assistant stage manager was Annette Verga-Lagier; the assistant director was Zetna Fuentes; the dramaturg was Francine Volpe; the general manager was Toni Marie Davis; and casting was by Jack Doulin. The cast was as follows:

WENDELL .... EJ Caroll
FLOYD .... Michael Imperioli
LINA .... Sharon Angela
GERONIMO .... Raul Aranas
FELIX .... Lazaro Perez
ROSALIND .... Quincy Tyler Bernstine

CHARACTERS

WENDELL, An unhealthy man

FLOYD, His longtime friend, wiry

LINA, Wendell's wife, six and half months pregnant

GERONIMO, A Filipino neighbor

FELIX, Floyd's dad

ROSALIND, Floyd's estranged wife

PLACE

The Bronx, not far from Fordham Road and Webster Avenue.

TIME

Present day.

CHICKEN

SCENE 1

Setting: A cramped apartment in the Bronx. Early afternoon.
At rise: Across much of the down and mid-stage — stacked
both ankle and knee-high — are piles of envelopes, piles of
papers, and several piles of junk. Wendell, an unhealthy look-
ing man, stares at a rooster, which sits in a cage below him.
Floyd, his friend, stands nearby.

WENDELL. *(To Floyd.)* He's a little sick. So he has to stay down-
stairs for a little while.
FLOYD. OK.
WENDELL. Yeah. Once he's better, he'll go on the roof. With the
other ones. Upstairs.
FLOYD. Other ones?
WENDELL. There are four more of them. On the roof.
FLOYD. Lina is gonna kill you.
WENDELL. The healthy ones are in the homing pigeon cages
right now. But he's 'spose to be the best one, why isn't he healthy
Floyd?
FLOYD. You need to get this bird out of the apartment.
WENDELL. He might die if he goes outside right now.
FLOYD. He's sitting here being sick in your living room.
WENDELL. So?
FLOYD. What if he gives us what he's got? What if he dies in here?
WENDELL. Why are you saying that?
FLOYD. Look at him. You can't just bring these things into your
home. He's so sick, they've got stuff on them.
WENDELL. You don't know that.
FLOYD. Didn't you at least ask why he looks so bad?

WENDELL. I think it happens sometimes.

FLOYD. Yeah. It just happens sometimes when you die. Why didn't you ask me about it before you bought it?

WENDELL. I didn't buy it.

FLOYD. Then where'd you get this thing?

WENDELL. Geronimo.

FLOYD. *(Beat.)* What?

WENDELL. Geronimo.

FLOYD. You're kiddin', right?

WENDELL. Look, I know you're still pissed at him.

FLOYD. Pissed at him?

WENDELL. You gotta get over this, Floyd.

FLOYD. *Pissed at him?* He's the reason I'm in this situation in the first place.

WENDELL. All you had to do was patch up old tires and help him raise chickens in the back.

FLOYD. He should be deported.

WENDELL. Look, I'm sorry he fired you, but welcome to one of his birds. *(Beat.)* Floyd. You know you can stay here as long as you want, but like … you can't, either.

FLOYD. My dad would think you're insane bringin' a bird in the house.

WENDELL. Speakin' of your dad —

FLOYD. I was not speakin' of my dad —

WENDELL. I called him up. He gave me a recipe to condition this thing. Like a diet plan. He said you'd know how to put it together right.

FLOYD. You called him up?

WENDELL. Yeah. He sorta ran out of juice towards the end, I didn't get the whole thing, and he's really hard to understand now, but he said you'd know how to administer it. Maybe you can call him up and get the rest of it. It's a morning-of thing, to get the birds excited before the fight.

FLOYD. Wendell?

WENDELL. What?

FLOYD. What are you doing?

WENDELL. *(Hard for him.)* Lina's about to pop with the baby, Floyd. You been loafin' on my couch for like three months. I got no fucking money left, her belly is getting bigger and bigger. You're gonna train this bird and then you're movin' out with the money.

FLOYD. *(Beat.)* Wendell. I got nowhere to go.

WENDELL. I'll help you find somewhere.

FLOYD. Wendell —

WENDELL. Thirty-five thousand if we win. You're the half Cuban, your people's DNA is built for this shit, you're the only person I know who even knows how to *look* at a fighting rooster.

FLOYD. Wendell —

WENDELL. It's in Washington Heights, Geronimo sucks at winning these things, he hasn't won since you left, you gotta do this Floyd. *(Beat.)* Then you gotta move out.

FLOYD. When your baby girl comes you're gonna ask yourself again and again why you didn't reach for that rubber two trimesters ago. A cockfight's not gonna help things.

WENDELL. Yeah it will.

FLOYD. This shit's illegal.

WENDELL. Illegal?

FLOYD. Don't you work for, like, the city?

WENDELL. So?

FLOYD. You should have ethics.

WENDELL. I collect tolls all day on the Whitestone Bridge. Ethics?

FLOYD. I got a strong feeling you're only shooting girl bullets.

WENDELL. Excuse me?

FLOYD. There is no doubt that your child is a girl. Look at the way you're behavin'. Take this piece-of-poultry-shit back to Geronimo and his smelly tire-pile-of-a-tire-shop and just let it go.

WENDELL. Floyd —

FLOYD. Filipino gypsy. He's gettin' in your head.

WENDELL. How?

FLOYD. Like he did. When we were kids.

WENDELL. He just wants you to show up to work on time.

FLOYD. Back of his tire shop hatchin' roosters so he can fight in Washington Heights? Filipinos: They do curses on you. He did his flip gypsy curse all over you and this bird. Putting his sad, third world face on, jealous we speak English *better,* I'm glad I quit his shop —

WENDELL. You got fired —

FLOYD. This bird's a mutt, look at it. It's sick. Any bird that's ever come outta the back a that shop that ever worked *I* built. I did not have a hand in this thing, I do not make sick birds.

WENDELL. Floyd.

FLOYD. What?

WENDELL. Apparently this thing is modified.

FLOYD. *(Beat.)* What?

WENDELL. He's enhanced. He's special.

FLOYD. What are you talkin' about?

WENDELL. Geronimo has added specifications. To his genes.

FLOYD. What? How?

WENDELL. He got a hold of some hormone. He put it in both bird's parents. His four brothers are just like him. Go look on the roof. They're huge. Plus you gotta see his moms.

FLOYD. *(Interested, but trying to hide it.)* She big?

WENDELL. His moms looks like Nell Carter.

FLOYD. What?

WENDELL. Yeah. Like *Gimme a Break.*

FLOYD. Wendell. Having a mom like Nell Carter, Wendell, I don' know if that's …

WENDELL. What?

FLOYD. Positive.

WENDELL. Sure it is.

FLOYD. Nell Carter's heart stopped at like forty.

WENDELL. *(Beat.)* Floyd. This thing's a Calagay.

FLOYD. A what?

WENDELL. A Calagay fighting rooster from Calagay, France.

FLOYD. France.

WENDELL. Yeah.

FLOYD. Like, Europe?

WENDELL. Yeah, like France. Calagay, France. *(Floyd examines the rooster more closely, perhaps approaching the cage.)*

FLOYD. France, huh?

WENDELL. Yeah. France.

FLOYD. How'd Nimo get him over here if he's from France?

WENDELL. Things from France are sophisticated.

FLOYD. Listen to you, you already *sound* like him.

WENDELL. Well it's true. France is classy.

FLOYD. You're a native born American and you just sounded like the City of Manila. "France is sophisticated," I can hear him sayin' it.

WENDELL. You walk outside today Floyd? Half of Haiti lives out there now there's so much French.

FLOYD. So?

8

WENDELL. You want to let these people to beat you? This is *your* country.

FLOYD. This country put me in an orphanage.

WENDELL. Poor fucking baby. Me too.

FLOYD. Don't we have enough roosters over here that we don't have to import them from France?

WENDELL. A chicken is a chicken.

FLOYD. *No.* A chicken is a girl chicken. A rooster is a boy chicken. All of them are birds. A chicken is not just a chicken, no wonder Geronimo conned you.

WENDELL. Cut his feathers, Floyd. We're gonna at least make him look good if he's gonna get his ass kicked.

FLOYD. That's the entirely wrong attitude to have, you thinking he's gonna get his ass kicked.

WENDELL. Cut his feathers like a fighting bird then I'll think whatever you want. I'll get you vitamins and supplements, you're gonna cut his feathers, you're gonna train this bird, then you're moving out.

FLOYD. No I'm not.

WENDELL. Yes you are.

FLOYD. I'm staying right here.

WENDELL. Stop pretending like you live here.

FLOYD. I do live here.

WENDELL. No. You. Don't. *(Pause.)*

FLOYD. *(A bit scared.)* You're serious.

WENDELL. Like a big piece of cancer. *(Another pause. Floyd examines the bird some more.)*

FLOYD. I gotta say.

WENDELL. What?

FLOYD. It's a very handsome rooster.

WENDELL. *(Beat.)* It is, isn't it?

FLOYD. Yeah. So he's modified.

WENDELL. Yeah. He's modified. From another continent. *(Beat.)* Floyd, I am so not fucking around with this. *(Beat.)* I'm going to get something to eat. I'm starving.

FLOYD. We just ate.

WENDELL. I'm hungry.

FLOYD. How?

WENDELL. I appreciate it, you cutting his feathers.

FLOYD. No problem.

WENDELL. These things are so depressing until somebody cuts their feathers.

FLOYD. Probably gonna be depressing afterwards too.

WENDELL. No. From here on out we talk positive. I'm goin' to get food. That's positive. Five French birds. That's positive. This chicken —

FLOYD. Rooster —

WENDELL. The rooster. Is positive. The entire planet is going to be a radioactive glow of positivity from here on out, okay?

FLOYD. *(Beat.)* OK.

WENDELL. Thank you for agreeing to cut his feathers.

FLOYD. No problem.

WENDELL. Just make sure you do it on the roof.

SCENE 2

Setting: The apartment. The same day. Late afternoon. At rise: The rooster looks different now, its feathers have been impressively cut. A bag of McDonald's sits on the kitchen table. Lina, Wendell's pregnant wife, keeps a safe distance from the rooster. She cannot believe what she is seeing. Wendell tries to explain.

LINA. *Are you kidding me?*

WENDELL. I was gonna move it. Why are you home so early?

LINA. 'Cause I'm pregnant. 'Cause my ankles hurt. 'Cause I threatened to sue Macy's if they didn't let me take a car service home for a minute — *why is there a rooster in my living room?*

WENDELL. You gotta go back again *tonight?*

LINA. How many times I gotta tell you: Perfume is eternal. *(Back to the rooster.)* What the fuck is this?

WENDELL. I can explain.

LINA. You better.

WENDELL. I brought it home for Floyd, so he'd train it and move out with the money.

LINA. They completely carry bacteria.

WENDELL. Who?

LINA. Birds.

WENDELL. No they don't. Where'd you hear that?

LINA. Move him outta the way. I gotta get to the kitchen.

WENDELL. You can get around it, just walk around him.

LINA. Him?

WENDELL. It's a boy.

LINA. There's shit everywhere, I got enough shit cluttering up my life, move *it*.

WENDELL. *(Referring to the piles.)* These are all *your* coupons and mailings.

LINA. So?

WENDELL. Who's cluttering who?

LINA. Half this shit is yours.

WENDELL. *(Pointing to one pile.)* That pile is the things you're saving up for, it's the coupons *you've* been cutting out; *(Pointing to another pile.)* that pile is a bunch of contest envelopes for free Florida vacations you asked me to keep; *(Pointing to another pile.)* that pile is a pile of strange bills I found in your *underwear drawer. (Realizing the frustration is over everything* but *the piles.)* Lina, I meant to move the bird upstairs, and then you came home, I'm sorry —

LINA. He's staring at me.

WENDELL. I'll go put him on the roof with the other four. He's only down here 'cause Nimo said he's sick.

LINA. *There are four more of these things?*

WENDELL. *(Changing the subject.)* You didn't take some money off my dresser this morning, did you?

LINA. No.

WENDELL. Y'know, just to, like, get to work?

LINA. I take it from your bank account — there's a chicken in our living room.

WENDELL. Seventy-five bucks was missing.

LINA. *(Knowing it was Floyd.)* I don't know why you're talkin' to me.

WENDELL. I'll move him upstairs.

LINA. Please get it moved before I get home tonight.

WENDELL. *(Assuredly.)* I will totally take care of this by the time you get home tonight, promise.

LINA. Where's Floyd?

WENDELL. Out botherin' somebody else for a change. *(Beat.)* We should make out. While we got the chance.

LINA. What?

WENDELL. You wanna make out?

LINA. *(Not too into the idea, still focused on the rooster.)* You wanna?

WENDELL. I mean, when again are we gonna get the chance?

LINA. How long's he been gone? You think he's looking for work?

WENDELL. If he is, we should celebrate. By making out.

LINA. *(Referring to the rooster.)* He's gonna stare at us while we do it.

WENDELL. No he won't. *(Sensing her reluctance.)* You should eat your McDonald's.

LINA. No.

WENDELL. OK.

LINA. The last thing I wanted to eat tonight was McDonald's.

WENDELL. Thought you liked McDonald's.

LINA. No, *you* like McDonald's. Ever since I got pregnant I'll tell you one thing: Your baby doesn't like McDonald's.

WENDELL. What?

LINA. Yeah.

WENDELL. You gotta eat somethin'. Floyd says Rosalind ate like a warthog when she was pregnant.

LINA. I don't care what that ho ate.

WENDELL. Jeez.

LINA. What I say about talkin' about her?

WENDELL. OK.

LINA. Pumpin' out babies like a fire hose.

WENDELL. She has *two* kids.

LINA. Taking up with another man while Floyd's at work. Don't get married if you don't want to get married, but don't bring home another man.

WENDELL. He cheated on her *forever.*

LINA. There is something wrong with women who do that. What if I did that to you? Took up with another man just 'cause you couldn't afford to pay the bills?

WENDELL. I pay the bills.

LINA. And what if you couldn't?

WENDELL. And you brought a man home?

LINA. Yeah. You'd call me a ho.

WENDELL. No I wouldn't.

LINA. And how does he NOT know that that oldest child is not his?

WENDELL. You gotta shut up with this.

LINA. I think he knows, he just doesn't give a shit. I mean c'mon. Theo — asthma, practically retarded — of course that's Floyd's kid, but Michael? I mean, c'mon.

WENDELL. Shut up.

LINA. Don't ever talk about Rosalind again in this house.

WENDELL. Fine. Then quiet about the kids.

LINA. Do not. Talk. About her.

WENDELL. OK. *(Wendell sour burps, a result of devouring his last meal too fast. He bangs his chest to regulate his misbehaving chest cavity; it looks uncomfortable.)*

LINA. You all right?

WENDELL. Yeah. Just ate too fast.

LINA. *(Curious.)* You ate already?

WENDELL. Yeah.

LINA. *(Concerned.)* Wendell?

WENDELL. What?

LINA. Nothin'.

WENDELL. What?

LINA. *(Trying to put this delicately, regarding Wendell.)* Were you a … healthy baby?

WENDELL. Why?

LINA. You weren't, were you?

WENDELL. My mom was fat and then she died. She forgot to mention it on the way to foster care.

LINA. I'm only asking. Wendell. It's just. I'm older.

WENDELL. I know. Eat some food. You're gonna be fine. You look great. *(Beat.)* This thing's gonna make us money.

LINA. *(Admiring the rooster.)* I never knew you could cut a rooster's feathers like that.

WENDELL. It's supposed to scare the other bird, when they fight.

LINA. Oh. *(Beat.)* I think I need to go to the bathroom. *(Lina exits into the bathroom. Wendell examines the rooster for a moment, unsure.)*

WENDELL. *(To the rooster.)* For what's it's worth, rooster. At least everyone agrees you're a good-lookin' bird. *(Wendell crosses to the table and takes out a McDonald's burger from the bag. He takes a bite. Still to the rooster:)* Thank God McDonald's still knows what they're doing. We may be all fucked up, guns and violence and bombs, but at least we can count on Mickey D's. Bullshit my kid doesn't like this food. *(The sound of keys in the door lock. The door opens. Floyd enters, carrying shopping bags.)*

FLOYD. You eatin' again?

WENDELL. Shut up.

FLOYD. Somebody smokin' in here?

WENDELL. No. *(Floyd crosses to the bathroom door and opens it. Behind the door, Lina — not going to the bathroom — is smoking a cigarette.)*

FLOYD. Why you sittin' on the toilet?

WENDELL. Lina.

LINA. What?

WENDELL. What are you doing?

LINA. Smoking.

WENDELL. Jesus.

LINA. What?

WENDELL. You're pregnant.

LINA. People in Ireland do it all the time.

WENDELL. Camilla tell you that too?

LINA. Yeah.

WENDELL. What I tell you about taking advice from the Irish?

LINA. She's half Irish.

FLOYD. Lina. What you're doing. That's not good.

WENDELL. If you didn't want the baby. You just had to tell me.

LINA. Maybe. I am.

WENDELL. *(Gathering himself.)* Gimme one a those cigarettes.

LINA. *(Concerned by this.)* I don't think you should.

WENDELL. You're tellin' *me* how *I* should live? Gimme one.

LINA. *(Handing Wendell the entire pack.)* You can have the whole pack. I have a whole carton in the closet. I had a coupon. *(Beat.)* You worked so hard to quit.

WENDELL. *(To Floyd, lighting up a cigarette.)* What do you got in that bag?

FLOYD. Groceries.

WENDELL. Excuse me?

FLOYD. Groceries.

WENDELL. Where'd you get money to buy groceries?

FLOYD. America's economy is pickin' up.

WENDELL. Yeah. Pickin' up off my dresser.

FLOYD. I thought you left it for me.

WENDELL. What else could you possibly need? I buy you beer. We buy you food. You're a *grown* man and you *get a stipend*. What is wrong with you, taking shit from me?

FLOYD. I bought shit for the bird.

WENDELL. *(Surprised and pleased.)* What?

FLOYD. Rooster supplies.

WENDELL. Really?

FLOYD. Yeah.

WENDELL. Lemme see.

FLOYD. Lina. Get off the toilet seat lid and come join us. I bought shit.

LINA. I'm fine here. *(Floyd studies Lina.)*

FLOYD. Lina.

LINA. What.

FLOYD. Lina. I gotta say.

LINA. What, Floyd. What do you gotta to say.

FLOYD. I gotta say, despite you sittin' on the toilet and your crappy dress and your hair. And your pregnancy.

LINA. What?

FLOYD. I think. You look very beautiful today.

WENDELL. Excuse me?

FLOYD. Very very beautiful. You are. Today.

LINA. *(Flustered but not unflattered.)* Well, thank you, Floyd.

WENDELL. Floyd. I'm standin' *right* here. That's my wife.

FLOYD. *(To Wendell.)* I know. It's just she looks very attractive. I mean, the dress could use some tailoring. But I always thought she was really pretty.

WENDELL. What the fuck is the matter with you?

LINA. I gotta get ready for work now. *(To Floyd.)* Thank you Floyd. For the compliment. *(Lina exits the bathroom, enters the living room, then exits into the bedroom.)*

FLOYD. *(To Lina as she exits, referring to Wendell.)* Make this guy go work extra time at the toll booth. You shouldn't be workin'. You should just be lookin' good.

WENDELL. *(To Floyd.)* What the fuck is wrong with you?

FLOYD. *(To Lina, now in the other room.)* I'm doing better, Lina. I am. Days ain't like they used to be anymore. I'm training this bird now. No need for you to go to work. Not after this thing starts winning. *(To Wendell.)* She shouldn't be working pregnant.

WENDELL. When you write a book on relationship advice and become a famous advice columnist, then I'll take your advice.

FLOYD. What? I'm feeling good. I'm not allowed to feel good?

WENDELL. No. Not when you don't got a job. Not when you say shit like that to my wife. Gimme me what's left of my money back.

FLOYD. I spent it all.

WENDELL. Gimme it.

FLOYD. I bought a lotta shit. *(Floyd takes out a jar of pickles from the grocery bag.)* Here. I bought you pickles. Trust me. Feed them to her in her time of need. 'Cause if her pregnancy is anything like Rosalind's was. *Fuck. (Beat.)* I called my dad up.

WENDELL. What?

FLOYD. Yeah. Long distance on your phone. While you were out.

WENDELL. What he say?

FLOYD. He gave me some recipes. To condition the cock.

WENDELL. That's great.

FLOYD. *(Taking out a slip of paper.)* His voice was very irritating. Took him like a half-an-hour to spit this out. I'm glad he has trouble talkin' now. *(Floyd hands Wendell the recipe.)*

WENDELL. This is fantastic.

FLOYD. That's the magic piece of paper. It's a little different from the one we used as kids. I think.

WENDELL. Why? Get the old one.

FLOYD. He's so protective of it. I couldn't sit on that phone anymore.

WENDELL. You got *all* day.

FLOYD. Geronimo and me never used old school recipes anyway.

WENDELL. I'm the one paying for all this shit, get the old one.

FLOYD. No.

WENDELL. *(Reading.)* What the fuck is D-Extract?

FLOYD. Part of the recipe.

WENDELL. For what?

FLOYD. We gonna make like a solvent. It's got ingredients from the orient in it. Soya bean oil, stewed tomatoes, jockey oats. It's like a paste, we are gonna make it now. Crude protein.

WENDELL. Not now we're not, not with her here.

FLOYD. This bird was your fucking idea.

WENDELL. We're waitin' till she's gone.

FLOYD. When she's gone *(Removing medical tubing from the bag.)* we'll teach Calagay to jump rope, run fast, keep his head back away from claws, get used to blades on his left talons, 'cause Christ knows it's too late to dub him, he'll never heal in time.

WENDELL. Dub him?

FLOYD. Cut the waddle and comb.

WENDELL. What the fuck is a waddle and comb?

FLOYD. The extra crap around his face, the skin. I mean groom-

16

ing, grooming is like an afterthought at this point. We're gonna discover the truth about how hard Geronimo conned you.

WENDELL. Floyd.

FLOYD. What?

WENDELL. Don't ever take money off my dresser again.

FLOYD. I'll do whatever the fuck I want.

WENDELL. No you won't.

FLOYD. Don't talk down to me.

WENDELL. What the hell is the matter with you?

FLOYD. Comin' in here with a rooster, telling me what I gotta do. You'd a been *dead* if it wasn't for me. You owe me a lot more than just seventy-five dollars. I'll take shit off your dresser whenever I want.

WENDELL. I repaid you plenty.

FLOYD. Wendell. There is no amount of money in the world that could repay me for the amount of beating and raping I saved you from in that boy's home. Do you know why you're able to put together a normal life in your adulthood? Because of me. Your life is better now because *I* allowed it to become better by using my brain to keep us both safe. And sacrificing for you. Because I love you. I'm the one who said you should go for Lina. You take her away from everybody, don't think Rosalind's not pissed they don't talk anymore. You never could get laid before without my help and now you're on Easy Street. Because I love you and I use my mind to help you. And now I'm gonna try to use that *same* mind to win us tens of thousands of dollars. With five crappy ass birds. All of which are your idea. But even then it'll be me who did it, who kept us safe, and protected everything. 'Cause I know how much money you got in the can. About zero, and don't think I don't know about how Lina don't know about how little money you have. Don't talk to me about seventy-five dollars again. That is just a speck on a cosmic chart of an infinite set of owing that you owe me. Don't ever embarrass me in front of your wife again. *(Beat.)* Now, once Lina goes to work. I expect you to be quiet and respectful while we put this shit together. You want a fighting bird, I'll give you a fighting bird. You just gotta get outta my way.

WENDELL. Fine. As soon as Geronimo leaves.

FLOYD. What?

WENDELL. He's coming over.

FLOYD. No. Call him up. Tell him he's not welcome. I got enough weak people in my life.

WENDELL. This is *my* house.

FLOYD. And it's mine too until I'm gone.

SCENE 3

Setting: The apartment. Early evening, about an hour later. At rise: Floyd standing with Geronimo, a Filipino man in a mechanic's uniform. Wendell is sitting. All three examine the bird, which looks a little sicker than before. On the kitchen counter sits a brown lunch bag containing something substantial.

GERONIMO. Calagay?

WENDELL. Yeah.

GERONIMO. Wendell: Calagary.

WENDELL. What?

GERONIMO. Calagary. Canada.

FLOYD. Canada?

GERONIMO. Why did you think he was from France?

WENDELL. 'Cause that's what you told me.

GERONIMO. No. I told you France is very sophisticated. I told you it would be nice to have a bird from the famous cock fighting town of Calagay, France. But this bird is from Calagary, Canada.

FLOYD. *(Correcting Geronimo.)* Calgary. Fucking Calgary. Say it.

GERONIMO. Calgary.

FLOYD. How hard was that?

GERONIMO. *(Serious.)* Floyd. I am going to say something to both you two gentlemen: These birds are perhaps the greatest gift you will ever receive from anybody. If you do not win, you will probably not win anything ever again in your whole lives.

FLOYD. *(To Geronimo.)* I checked on his jumping ability and his agility and he didn't do shit, he is slow as concrete. You're not a very good breeder anymore, Nimo. Have you chorded him even? Have you even *tried* to harden him?

GERONIMO. Sort of.

FLOYD. What about his brothers?

GERONIMO. Sort of.

FLOYD. At least his eyes are clean. He flips okay, but I doubt he can be properly pointed in time, we gotta hope he's got instinct. He ever sparred?

GERONIMO. No.

FLOYD. Fuck. Of course not. You haven't been the same since your wife died.

GERONIMO. Fuck you.

FLOYD. Leave.

GERONIMO. Floyd. God is looking down on you. He is judging your ability to be of any value to anybody. He is asking you why you do not have a job. He is asking why you are a terrible father. He is asking why he brought you into this world. God is wondering this, Floyd.

FLOYD. *(To Wendell.)* Get him outta here.

WENDELL. No.

GERONIMO. But at least you cut his feathers well.

WENDELL. Floyd always cuts feathers well.

GERONIMO. *(Perhaps referring to the bowl on the counter.)* But this paste you made, this paste was a bad idea.

FLOYD. *(To Wendell.)* Get him outta here.

WENDELL. No. He bred them. He built them. He's the only one with a minivan.

FLOYD. *(Turning his attention towards Geronimo.)* Nimo. If these birds are the best then why did one of his brothers die?

GERONIMO. *(Beat.)* What?

FLOYD. Yeah. One of his brothers died.

GERONIMO. When?

FLOYD. Just before you got here.

WENDELL. I found him on the roof. I gave him a little impromptu burial, put him in a brown paper lunch bag. *(Pointing to the brown paper bag.)* That's him over there.

FLOYD. Your birds can't even survive on a rooftop in regular weather.

GERONIMO. Motherfucker.

WENDELL. We are gonna need another one of his brothers from his tire shop.

FLOYD. Tell me you got a backup brother. *(Beat.)* Tell me you bred a couple more than just five, right?

GERONIMO. Of course I did.

FLOYD. Well that's good.

GERONIMO. Floyd.

FLOYD. What?

GERONIMO. Tell me you still have your knives. Every other blade we had broke at the last fight. *(Taking a blade out of his pocket and placing it on the table.)* I only have one Mexican short knife left.

FLOYD. So?

GERONIMO. Tell me you still have your knives. *(Beat.)* Floyd.

FLOYD. What?

GERONIMO. Where is your set of bird knives?

FLOYD. *(Crossing to the table, picking up the Mexican short knife.)* I sold them. I don't have them.

GERONIMO. Oh boy. OK.

FLOYD. Maybe you should think twice before cutting back on your workforce.

GERONIMO. You never came to work. How could you be considered part of my workforce?

FLOYD. Bet you could sure use my knives now.

GERONIMO. You have to sweet talk to your father. We need his Cubano knives. We need his recipe.

FLOYD. Fuck you.

GERONIMO. Your father is going to be dead soon anyway.

FLOYD. So?

GERONIMO. He is probably going to leave them to you. Just get them early.

FLOYD. He's not going to leave them to me.

WENDELL. Nimo, don't talk about his dad being dead.

GERONIMO. Floyd. One more time, let's do this thing, I raise, you train, we win a lot of money. You can move out. Wendell doesn't have to give Rosalind money for the children. We are all happy. *(Beat.)*

FLOYD. What?

WENDELL. Nimo.

FLOYD. *(Stunned.)* What?

GERONIMO. *(To Floyd.)* Give this poor guy a break. Let's win money for him.

FLOYD. *(To Wendell.)* When you do that?

WENDELL. *(To Geronimo.)* Why'd you say that?

FLOYD. *(To Wendell.)* When you do that?

WENDELL. *(To Floyd.)* When *didn't* I do that?

FLOYD. She doesn't need money.

GERONIMO. *(Sarcastic.)* OK, she doesn't.

WENDELL. What the fuck did you think was going on? You thought you were paying all your bills selling roosters and patching tires for a living? Rosalind can't hold a steady job. I just thought you were just too embarrassed to say anything.

FLOYD. *(To Wendell.)* You really been doin' that?

WENDELL. Floyd, of course I have. What else am I supposed to do?

GERONIMO. Go see your father.

FLOYD. Shut up. *(Beat, to Wendell.)* You really been doin' that?

WENDELL. Floyd. She was in a really bad place for a while.

GERONIMO. *(Focused.)* Floyd. Honestly. I could give a shit about your kids. Get your father's recipe. Take my minivan. Get the morning-of recipe, then get his knives. Then fuck him in the face for me.

FLOYD. *(Touched?)* You really wanna lend me your minivan?

GERONIMO. Yes.

FLOYD. OK.

GERONIMO. I suppose you are going to need the money for the tolls too?

WENDELL. It's like twenty-five bucks for tolls.

FLOYD. *(Exploding, totally crazy.) I don't ever wanna hear about you motherfuckers ever giving Rosalind money again. (To Geronimo.) Yes* I need twenty five dollars. Yes I need your keys. I'm gonna drive up there tonight, I'm gonna fuckin' camp out, and I'll take that fucker to the dog track first thing. 'Cause this is gonna take work. This is gonna take convincing. You want a recipe, I'll give you a recipe. You want knives, I'll get you knives. Don't ever give Rosalind money again. Give me the keys.

GERONIMO. *(Giving Floyd the keys.)* Here.

FLOYD. *(Taking them.)* Now give me the twenty-five bucks.

SCENE 4

Scene: The apartment. Later that night. At rise: The television is tuned to a talk show, of the self-help variety. Lina is seated on the La-Z-Boy. Still in her work attire, she is opening mail. A beer sits unopened nearby. She takes a cigarette out of a pack and lights it, then regards the rooster

LINA. *(To the rooster.)* You don't mind if I smoke, do you bird? *(She takes a big drag. She opens another piece of mail. To the rooster, referring to the opened piece of mail:)* Oh look, we won another car. *(Beat.)* I'd give away Mazdas too if I had them. *(She takes another drag, then opens more mail. She reads with a distant ennui.)* Why didn't we pay this? *(Lifting up another envelope, perhaps holding it up to the light to see its contents, but not about to open it, then perhaps to the rooster.)* If that last statement made me sad, this Visa bill's gonna make me suicidal. *(Then prompted by subject matter being talked about on the television.)* You married bird? "Do you still love *your* spouse?" *(She puts the envelope down, then opens the can of beer, taking a sip. She stares at the rooster, perhaps guiltily. Defensively, to the rooster:)* People in Ireland do it all the time.

SCENE 5

Setting: The stadium-style seats at the greyhound track in Bridgeport, Connecticut. The next day. At rise: Floyd sitting with his dad, Felix, who is old and suffering from a condition; the left half of his body does not respond well and his speech is slurred. As much as possible, Felix's responses come from nodding and motioning, but he cannot resist the urge to speak.

FELIX. He.
FLOYD. He what? What did *he* do?

FELIX. He.

FLOYD. C'mon Broken Brain. Formulate a new sentence, I know you got another thought in there, fight through this, what'd the nurse say.

FELIX. He. Called. Me.

FLOYD. You didn't have to answer.

FELIX. *(Again, not wanting to say it again, trying to say something else.)* He. Called. Me.

FLOYD. I know. You told me.

FELIX. *(One more time, then embarrassed.)* He.

FLOYD. He what? Jesus.

FELIX. He's. A good kid. Wendell.

FLOYD. He is, huh?

FELIX. Wendell's. A. Good. Kid.

FLOYD. Then what am I?

FELIX. You. Are. A. Good kid too.

FLOYD. Even though you got mush mouth I can still tell you lie. *(Pause.)*

FELIX. Where. Is. Geronimo?

FLOYD. Playing with used Goodyear radials in the Boogie Down Bronx like a child, what do you care?

FELIX. *(Clearly trying to ask something else.)* Wendell. Called. Me.

FLOYD. You're, like, trapped in there, aren't you? You were talkin' about something else, and now you're, just, back to the old thought.

FELIX. I. Am. Learning. Wendell called me. *(Believing that he is saying a new thought, but only realizing after he has not.)* Wendell. Is. A. Good. Kid.

FLOYD. *Start over.* When that happens, *start over.* You were right there when the nurse said it. Do what she says or repeat like a recording your whole life. You were smart enough to desert me to cut down on expenses so you gotta be smart enough to try and start to talk normally for five seconds. *(Felix returns to his dog racing magazine, after a moment he tries to speak again.)*

FELIX. I. Hate. This.

FLOYD. Well I hate you, so imagine how I feel.

FELIX. Please. Be nice.

FLOYD. OK. I'm sorry. *(Beat.)* That recipe you gave me *sucked.* It made the bird sicker. *(Trying to be nice.)* What, what do you hate?

FELIX. What?

FLOYD. You said you "hate this," what do you hate?

FELIX. This.

FLOYD. The dog track, the fact that it's gonna rain, the fact you gotta beg Wendell and me for money when we barely got any, or the fact you got a stroke? Which one do you hate?

FELIX. *(Referring to his condition.)* This.

FLOYD. Well I'm sorry about it. I'm sure it's very frustrating.

FELIX. Thank-you. For. Coming.

FLOYD. No problem. Nimo lent me his car. It was no problem.

FELIX. Geronimo. Geronimo. *(Starting over.)* Is. A. Nice guy.

FLOYD. Yeah, for a flip he's a real nice guy.

FELIX. He. He. *(Focusing.)* Geronimo. Is. A nice guy.

FLOYD. This is a real boring conversation.

FELIX. He. Is. Filipino.

FLOYD. Yup. That's true. And he doesn't like you very much any-more. Look, *(Handing Felix a pad and pencil.)* give us the regimen. We could have some good birds here. One of them died, I brought him for you to take a look. But I still think they might be good. Maybe later you can show me how you used to fasten the Mexican short knife, he's still got it on. *(Referring to the dead rooster, perhaps showing the knife strapped to the talon.)* Please. For us. Give us the ingredients.

FELIX. You. You. Make it right?

FLOYD. What?

FELIX. The. The. Recipe. I gave you.

FLOYD. Pop. Course I did.

FELIX. No. No. I-bet-no.

FLOYD. I made what you told me to make.

FELIX. I bet. You made. It wrong.

FLOYD. Why? Why do you think that?

FELIX. How. How. How did you like. My nurse?

FLOYD. What?

FELIX. My nurse.

FLOYD. That nurse of yours is totally hot.

FELIX. She is totally. Hot. She, though. Is mean.

FLOYD. I'm gonna let you in on a secret: They're gonna keep on peeling away privileges at that home, first they'll be mean, then lights out at nine, then no TV, then no butter, then you die.

FELIX. *(Referring to the six-pack at Floyd's feet.)* Will. My. Medication?

FLOYD. What?

FELIX. Allow-me. To. To have a beer?

FLOYD. I don't know. Might be dangerous.

FELIX. Can. I. Have. A beer?

FLOYD. No.

FELIX. Why? Why not?

FLOYD. Captain Blood Clot, what's the magic word?

FELIX. *(Beat.)* Please.

FLOYD. There.

FELIX. *(Working hard.) Please.* Can-I. Have. A beer?

FLOYD. No. *(Felix returns to his dog racing paper. Floyd hands a beer to him. Felix stares at him helplessly.)*

FELIX. Please. Open. Bottle.

FLOYD. OK. *(Floyd does nothing.)*

FELIX. Please. *(Floyd opens the beer and hands the beer to Felix. Felix tries hard to take a sip but dribbles on himself.)*

FLOYD. If you're gonna dribble on yourself, you should use a straw.

FELIX. You have. One?

FLOYD. *(Removing a straw from the bag.)* Yes, I have one, I grabbed one from the package store. *(Beat.)* Why do they call them package stores up here?

FELIX. No.

FLOYD. I hate this state.

FELIX. No. I don't. Want a. Straw.

FLOYD. You sure? *(Felix nods.)* Suit yourself, Dribble Monster.

FELIX. How. How. Is. Rosalind?

FLOYD. She's a slut. I moved out.

FELIX. She is. She is nice.

FLOYD. No, she's not.

FELIX. How. Is. Theo?

FLOYD. Fine. He's got asthma now, but it's always something with him.

FELIX. Theo doesn't. Theo doesn't —

FLOYD. What?

FELIX. Visit.

FLOYD. He's five.

FELIX. Michael visits.

FLOYD. Stop making up shit.

FELIX. Michael. Visits. He visited.

FLOYD. When?

FELIX. He has. A junior high. Dance. Next week.

FLOYD. He visited? Here?

FELIX. Port Authority. He. Wanted. To talk.

FLOYD. Why?

FELIX. He. Is. A-good-kid.

FLOYD. He's gotten a little too chubby and a little too swishy for me.

FELIX. No.

FLOYD. Where the fuck he learn to take a bus?

FELIX. He is like you. When. When you were young. Traveling.

FLOYD. He wasn't put in an orphanage by a father who was too busy to care for him. So we're a little different like that. *(Felix drinks and dribbles on himself, as prophesied.)* Now that you've had your bath, *(Indicating the pen and paper.)* write down the *real* recipe we used for roosters, *before* the race starts. Don't you dare fuck with me. Pretend like you're writing out your will.

FELIX. Steroids?

FLOYD. What?

FELIX. Do. You. Want? Steroids?

FLOYD. Why would I want steroids?

FELIX. Recipes. With steroids. They-have. Steroid recipes. Now for birds.

FLOYD. Did we give birds steroids when I was young? *(Felix shakes his head no.)* Did we win when I was young? *(Felix shakes his head yes.)* Then *why* would I want steroids? Last thing I want is a more bulky bird.

FELIX. You-buy-them-at-the-vitamin-stores.

FLOYD. Even in that *(Referring to Felix's mind.)* lock box of a brain. You're still fuckin' with me.

FELIX. Mormons. Invented. Bird steroids.

FLOYD. Stop it. Dad.

FELIX. Mormons. Are into / roosters.

FLOYD. Stop / it.

FELIX. In Utah, Mormons in Utah — *(Floyd hits Felix hard.)*

FLOYD. You made me do that. You are *not allowed* to do that to me anymore. Write down the recipe, write down the *old* way. What we did when I was a kid. *(Fearing another strike, Felix begins to write furiously.)*

FELIX. *(Trying not to say this.)* Mormons —

FLOYD. STOP REPEATING THE THING YOU JUST GOT HIT FOR!

FELIX. *(Focusing.)* Please-don't. Hit me.

FLOYD. OK. I won't hit you. *(Beat.)* I'm sorry I hit you.

FELIX. OK. OK. *(Felix cowers, and stops writing. The starting bell of the gates opening sound, the race has begun, Felix pays attention although in pain.)*

FLOYD. Who'd you bet on?

FELIX. *(Starting over.)* I don't. Bet anymore. Watching. Is fine.

FLOYD. Watching doesn't sound like you.

FELIX. I. I like watching. I will-be. Adopting a dog.

FLOYD. You're going to be adopting a dog? Like a greyhound? Where you gonna put it?

FELIX. In. My house.

FLOYD. House?

FELIX. When I move. Out of. The center. When-I-get-better.

FLOYD. *(Now curious.)* When are you getting better?

FELIX. I will adopt. Even if. I don't. Get. Better. I will feed him. In the back yard. Of-the-center.

FLOYD. They're not going to let you do that.

FELIX. They. Might.

FLOYD. Want some rum?

FELIX. Yes.

FLOYD. Then finish writing.

FELIX. Don't. Hit me.

FLOYD. OK. *(Felix writes, then stops.)*

FELIX. I. Am. Done.

FLOYD. *(Handing Felix another beer.)* Here. Congrats. Have some rum, Drunken Master. *(Floyd opens it for Felix.)*

FELIX. Thank. Thank you.

FLOYD. No problem. *(Felix drinks it really fast, dribbling some, but getting most of it down. Referring to the race:)* Which one you pick to win?

FELIX. Five. Five.

FLOYD. *(Looking out, noticing the dog is ahead.)* Five is going to win.

FELIX. I know. That's why. I think. He will win. *(Number Five wins.)* See?

FLOYD. Yeah. *(Felix, it appears, is beginning to slump from the alcohol consumption.)*

FELIX. This rum. Tastes good.

FLOYD. Well I guess that's good then. You dirty Cuban. Gimme the recipe. *(Floyd grabs the recipe from Felix, opens himself a beer as if in celebration, then reads the slip of paper. After a moment, it becomes apparent that what is on the sheet of paper is seriously troubling to Floyd.)* Why would you write something like this? *(Felix has grown very nearly unconscious, perhaps blubbering a bit. Furious at the information on the note, Floyd takes out one of the last beers from the bag and pours it down Felix's flaccid throat. He throws the bottle to the ground, reaches into Felix's pockets, and takes out his wallet and removes his cash, ID's, and photographs. Beat: Floyd catches a glimpse of one of the photographs.)* Only you would have a photograph of a fucking greyhound and not one of your son. You pig. *(Taking the dead rooster — perhaps still in the bag — and throwing it in Felix's lap.)* Take this fuckin' rooster, hope the Connecticut cops shove the Mexican short knife up your ass. All I needed was your fuckin' advice. *(Perhaps hitting Felix hard with the dead rooster.)* Fuck you. And fuck your greyhound.

SCENE 6

> *Setting: The apartment. Later that night. At rise: Lina is sipping on a can of beer. Her cigarettes and lighter are in plain view. A knock is heard at the door. Lina takes a big swig from her beer and then throws it in the garbage. Another knock. Lina crosses to the door and presses her ear against the frame.*

LINA. Yes?

ROSALIND. *(Offstage.)* Lina. I need to ask you a question.

LINA. Who is this?

ROSALIND. *(Offstage.)* Who the fuck else would knock on your door at eleven at night?

LINA. Go away.

ROSALIND. *(Offstage.)* Lina, c'mon

LINA. Rosalind. Go away.

ROSALIND. *(Offstage.)* No. I'm just gonna keep on knockin'. *(Rosalind knocks three times, forcefully.)*

LINA. I thought hoes only walked the street.

ROSALIND. *(Offstage.)* Say something like that to my face with the door open. *(Beat.)* Can I talk to your husband?

LINA. Wendell's sleeping. If I let you in, by the time you take off your coat you'll have fucked him.

ROSALIND. *(Offstage; truly nice.)* Please. Angel, c'mon. Let me in.

LINA. *(Quietly.)* No.

ROSALIND. *(Offstage.)* Please. *(Beat.)* Lina. It's just me. *(Lina undoes the deadbolt and opens the door. Rosalind stands at the door, disheveled.)*

LINA. Make one fucking eye at Wendell while you're here and I'll stab your eye with scissors.

ROSALIND. Thank you for letting me in.

LINA. You look like shit girl.

ROSALIND. *(Referring to the bedroom.)* He sleeping in there?

LINA. What did I just say about talking about my husband?

ROSALIND. *(Meaning it.)* Sorry.

LINA. Why do you always want somebody else's things?

ROSALIND. Lina, I don't want your husband.

LINA. I don't see you for months, and now you're showing up here out of the blue at midnight? What else could you possibly want?

ROSALIND. Honey, when did you develop this whole paranoia thing?

LINA. When did you develop this whole *I'm busted* thing?

ROSALIND. Could you *try* and be nice? *(A beat as Lina considers this. Rosalind settles in, perhaps taking a seat. She notices the rooster.)* You got a. You got a bird in the house.

LINA. Get outta here.

ROSALIND. That's a big bird. This is an apartment building. You know that, right?

LINA. Leave.

ROSALIND. *(Recalling.)* Wait, oh shit, that, is that Nimo's bird?

LINA. You heard about it?

ROSALIND. Yeah. Why's it in your apartment?

LINA. It's sick. You really heard about it?

ROSALIND. Wow. That looks impressive.

LINA. You think so?

ROSALIND. Totally. You think it could win?

LINA. I don't know.

ROSALIND. Who gets the money if it does?

LINA. Why don't you *try* getting a job?

ROSALIND. That thing looks like it could kick some ass.

LINA. Rosalind.

ROSALIND. What?

LINA. What do you want?

ROSALIND. I need to talk to Wendell.

LINA. What do you got to talk to him about?

ROSALIND. Things.

LINA. I already got your husband living on my couch 'cause you couldn't keep your legs shut, you don't get to talk to Wendell about things.

ROSALIND. The dude was rich. Floyd does shit like this constantly. Tired a people callin' me a slut all the time.

LINA. Well then what would you like to be called?

ROSALIND. Practical. *(Beat.)* Eat some pickles. You're pregnant. You're emotional. How 'bout offering me something to drink?

LINA. We don't keep drinks in this house.

ROSALIND. In *this* house? Excuse me? Did I get lost in the hallway?

LINA. Rosalind, I'm tired, I just got home from work. Could you please leave?

ROSALIND. Lina?

LINA. What?

ROSALIND. Wendell was supposed to lend me some money.

LINA. Lend you money?

ROSALIND. This is hard enough. Don't make it harder.

LINA. Lend you money for what? We don't have any money.

ROSALIND. Can't believe you have a rooster in your house.

LINA. Don't change the subject.

ROSALIND. Michael's got his junior high dance thing coming up. And Theodore, with the asthma.

LINA. So?

ROSALIND. *(Looking around the apartment more, noticing the contest envelopes.)* What's with the contest envelopes? You win something recently?

LINA. No.

ROSALIND. You ever open up the paper and read about somebody who actually *won* those things?

LINA. *(Snapping.)* Why would Wendell give you money?

ROSALIND. *I don't know, I just need some now, can you give me some? He's been doing it for years.*

LINA. Years?

ROSALIND. Yeah, but since your belly started getting bigger, things have kind of dried up. Can I have that drink now? I'd even have some of that Black Velvet shit.

LINA. We don't keep liquor in this house.

ROSALIND. Give me one of my fuckin' husband's beers. I'm sure there's plenty in the fridge.

LINA. You're disgusting.

ROSALIND. I'm disgusting? You got a barnyard animal in your living room. You should start doing normal human stuff again. Like comin' out with the girls once in a while again.

LINA. Look what hanging out with you resulted in.

ROSALIND. It resulted in what used to be two really good friends. *(Lina opens the refrigerator. Several six packs of beer are visibly on display. In fact, besides the pickles and bird ingredients, nothing much else is in there. She grabs a beer and brings one to Rosalind, who opens it and takes a sip.)* Thank you. *(Beat.)* How's your dirty friend Camilla?

LINA. She's not dirty.

ROSALIND. Sure she's not. She still work at the same mother-fuckin' counter?

LINA. She works at a different counter now from when you worked there.

ROSALIND. *(Offers Lina some of her beer.)* Here. You should have one of these. Looks like you need it.

LINA. Rosalind, I'm pregnant.

ROSALIND. So was I, honey, so was I.

LINA. *No, I don't do that.*

ROSALIND. Think of it like this: You're giving baby a break from her day-to-day. It's like a vacation for your baby. I don't care what the doctor's say. *(Noticing the inexpensive cigarettes on the table.)* Shit, Lina, you're smokin' *those* now?

LINA. They're Wendell's.

ROSALIND. What, you have a coupon?

LINA. Yeah.

ROSALIND. Coupons. Jesus.

LINA. *(Beat.)* Michael's got a dance?

ROSALIND. Yeah. This whole "dance prom thing," it's kind of gay in this day and age, isn't it?

LINA. No.

ROSALIND. They get all dressed up, it's pretty gay.

LINA. Getting dressed up is kind of nice.

ROSALIND. Well, if you do it like Michael does it's gay. *(Beat.)*

Caught him in my bedroom the other day with that Indian kid.

LINA. Ravinder?

ROSALIND. Yeah. You know him? His parents got those blue turbans?

LINA. *Little* Ravinder?

ROSALIND. Little? He ain't little. No wonder Michael brought him home. Ravinder was so scared I was going to tell his Sikh parents.

LINA. Ravinder. *Really?*

ROSALIND. So much for Michael being young for his grade. *(Suddenly serious.)* Lina.

LINA. What?

ROSALIND. You gotta promise not to say anything to Floyd. Last thing that kid needs is Floyd telling him he's a mutant.

LINA. I swear. I won't. I promise.

ROSALIND. Ravinder's father would beat the crap outta him. Who knows what they keep in those turbans.

LINA. Lemme have a sip of your beer.

ROSALIND. What?

LINA. Can I have a sip of your beer?

ROSALIND. Honey, it's your beer. *(Lina takes the can from Rosalind and takes a substantial sip.)*

LINA. That tastes good.

ROSALIND. Drinking with a baby sometimes is the only way to go. Makes your titties stop hurting for a minute.

LINA. Rosalind.

ROSALIND. What?

LINA. I don't want to have this baby.

ROSALIND. You don't know what you're saying. All you gotta do is birth it —

LINA. Birth is gonna hurt —

ROSALIND. The rest will take care of itself. Drink your beer. *(Lina takes a substantial drink from the beer.)* Damn, honey.

LINA. I'm a little drunk.

ROSALIND. Floyd convinced you to put this bird in here, didn't he?

LINA. Wendell brought it home.

ROSALIND. Doesn't seem like a Wendell thing. *(The sound of Wendell stirring in the bedroom can be heard.)*

LINA. He's awake. He's gonna come to the refrigerator. *(Wendell enters groggily and heads to the refrigerator. He has obviously just thrown on a pair of pants for the trip.)*

WENDELL. Who you talking to?

LINA. Nobody.

ROSALIND. Hi Wendell.

LINA. Rosalind.

WENDELL. Rosalind?

ROSALIND. How you doing, baby?

WENDELL. What the fuck you doing here?

LINA. She came to borrow some money Wendell. You know anything about that?

WENDELL. *(To Rosalind.)* What I tell you about mentioning that to people.

ROSALIND. I didn't mention it to people. Until it stopped coming.

LINA. She says you been doing this since for years. That's a long time, honey. You never told me this when we got married.

WENDELL. You know what, Lina? I don't feel like I got an obligation to explain everything to everybody all the time. Especially not after midnight.

LINA. Wendell.

WENDELL. *(Snapping, cranky from being woken up.) I pay most of the bills around here! What's wrong with me doin' something that I thought was right?*

LINA. Are you tryin' to tell me something?

WENDELL. *If I told you you woulda made me stop doin' it,* calling her a slut all the time.

ROSALIND. Then why'd you stop doing it?

WENDELL. Have you *seen* my wife's belly? Have you noticed your husband doesn't come home to you anymore? *Have you noticed the male chicken in my living room?*

ROSALIND. You're like a big yeti in the morning.

WENDELL. *It's not the morning! It's fucking midnight* — *(To Lina, noticing the beer.)* Were you drinking a beer?

LINA. I had a half a one.

ROSALIND. Or eighty percent, but whatever.

WENDELL. *(To Lina.)* What the fuck is wrong with my life? Trying to do things right is, like, fucking useless. You said you wouldn't drink.

ROSALIND. Wendell, when you're upset, you're really really cute.

LINA. Fuck you Rosalind.

ROSALIND. *(To Lina.)* No. Fuck you. Don't talk to me like that. You got a good man and you're always treatin' him like shit.

Ungrateful bitch. *(Lina slaps Rosalind hard. Beat. Rosalind composes herself.)* You're lucky you got that belly. *(Rosalind exits into the bathroom.)*

WENDELL. Jesus. *(Absorbing it all, then gently.)* Lina.

LINA. What?

WENDELL. *(Beat.)* I need you to do me a favor.

LINA. No.

WENDELL. You're gonna go over to the stash a money that you keep in back of your closet and shove her like a hundred bucks. Just get her outta here. I need to go back to sleep.

LINA. I don't have a stash of money.

WENDELL. I see it every time I put on my slippers, yes you do.

LINA. You know about that?

WENDELL. I thought you deserved your privacy. Give her some money. Stop drinking. Give her what she wants.

LINA. What *she* wants? I want to go out on a Friday night, I *want* to not be saddled with debt like my mother, I want a decent non-fast food meal, you're the one who wants the baby. You're the one who wants a family, NO, you give her *your* money, I'm so sick of you making me feel bad. *(Rosalind exits from the bathroom. Almost simultaneously, keys are heard in the door as Floyd enters, looking rough.)*

ROSALIND. *(To Floyd.)* Hello Floyd.

FLOYD. *(To Rosalind.)* What the fuck are you doing here?

WENDELL. No, no, turn away and go back from where you came from, sleep in the minivan.

ROSALIND. Floyd. We were just talking about how good-looking you used to be.

FLOYD. You have a whole apartment, go home. I'm already killing these people.

ROSALIND. Maybe you should have thought of that before you were the worst father on the planet for twelve years.

FLOYD. *(To Wendell.)* Get her out of here.

WENDELL. No.

LINA. Floyd.

FLOYD. What?

LINA. Did you cut a bird's feathers in the bathtub?

FLOYD. Yeah. Why? That's not right?

LINA. You can't cut them on the Earth outside?

FLOYD. Next time I will.

ROSALIND. He's lying.

FLOYD. SHUT UP.

ROSALIND. *NO.*

FLOYD. *(To Wendell, handing him a slip of paper.)* Look what my dad wrote. *(Wendell takes the piece of paper and reads. To Rosalind:)* You know Michael's been to visit my dad?

ROSALIND. Yes.

WENDELL. *(Referring to the note.)* He wrote this?

FLOYD. *(To Rosalind.)* Maybe you shoulda told me he was visiting him?

ROSALIND. What's this sudden concern for your kids?

WENDELL. Michael visited Felix?

FLOYD. *(To Wendell.)* You believe that?

ROSALIND. He deserves to do what he wants.

WENDELL. He's twelve years old. What he do, take a bus?

ROSALIND. Somebody's gotta visit him.

FLOYD. What kind of mother are you?

ROSALIND. It drops him off *right there.*

WENDELL. *(Reading the note, disbelief.)* What the fuck is this? He really wrote this?

FLOYD. You know anything about that Wendell?

WENDELL. Jesus Christ.

LINA. What?

FLOYD. You gotta read this Lina, it is very interesting. *(Lina crosses to Wendell and reads the slip of paper.)*

ROSALIND. Lemme see. *(Rosalind grabs the note and reads it.)*

FLOYD. *(To Rosalind.)* What's that all about? Something you want to tell me?

ROSALIND. Floyd, you know that note's not true.

WENDELL. *(Discovering a wallet amidst Floyd's possessions on the counter.)* What's this?

FLOYD. I had to take his wallet to preserve his stuff, to keep it from dropping all over, he dribbled everywhere. You can probably see beer on the paper, it went all over.

WENDELL. *(Realizing.)* What's he gonna do without his wallet?

FLOYD. If I were governor of a state I'd make dog tracks illegal.

ROSALIND. Floyd.

FLOYD. What?

ROSALIND. *(Putting something together.)* Why do you have his wallet?

FLOYD. I don't know. I had to take it from him.

WENDELL. *(Putting something together too.)* Floyd.

FLOYD. What?

WENDELL. Why the fuck do you got Felix's wallet?

FLOYD. He should be giving us money.

WENDELL. His license in there? *(Rosalind picks up the wallet and examines the contents.)*

FLOYD. Yeah, so?

ROSALIND. And so are his pictures.

FLOYD. Notice not a single photo of his grandchildren.

ROSALIND. Do *you* have any photos of your kids in *your* wallet?

FLOYD. No. I'm not their grandfather. Notice the photo of the fucking greyhound he wants to buy?

ROSALIND. Please tell me you didn't do what I think you did.

LINA. What?

FLOYD. I don't know what you're talking about.

ROSALIND. Sure you do.

WENDELL. No.

LINA. What?

WENDELL. *(Now knowing.)* Please tell me you didn't.

LINA. *What?*

WENDELL. Floyd.

ROSALIND. Jesus.

FLOYD. *What?*

WENDELL. You fucking grandpa-dumped him?

LINA. What?

ROSALIND. Floyd.

LINA. "Grandpa-dumped"?

ROSALIND. Jesus.

LINA. What's he talking about?

FLOYD. Nothing. Ignore them.

LINA. You left your dad at the track?

FLOYD. Not really.

LINA. He's in Connecticut all alone?

FLOYD. It's his home. *(Referring to the wallet.)* See? He's even got a Connecticut driver's license.

LINA. Don't you think he might need it?

ROSALIND. You're nasty.

LINA. I'm going to lay down. *(Lina begins to head to the bedroom.)*

FLOYD. You know, it's a real misnomer, "grandpa-dumped." He's not *my* grandpa.

WENDELL. *He's Theo's grandpa, he's Michael's grandpa!*
FLOYD. Yeah? Is he Wendell? *(Lina enters the bedroom.)*
ROSALIND. No wonder your boys are all fucked up.
WENDELL. You're terrifying. Gimme the fucking keys to the car. What bleacher you leave him in?
FLOYD. I forgot.
WENDELL. Fuck you. I'm going to get the recipe.
FLOYD. One hundred miles away and the Bridgeport park closed at nine. I'd say tomorrow'd be the day for that.
WENDELL. The cockfight's tomorrow. Hope you get fucking arrested.
FLOYD. You have no idea how expensive he was.
WENDELL. Expensive.
FLOYD. Emotionally expensive. *(Wendell takes two leftover hamburgers out of the refrigerator, wraps them in a paper towel, and puts them in his pocket.)*
FLOYD. What's that for?
WENDELL. The road.
FLOYD. You eat too much.
WENDELL. You leave old men at the track too much.
ROSALIND. Wendell, I just want to leave. Michael's got a dance.
WENDELL. So?
ROSALIND. Don't do this to me.
WENDELL. I don't care what Michael's got. He's goin' with a boy anyway. *I'm outta money.* Tell Michael to get a job. He might be gay, but he's the most equipped man I know at this point. Or you could try showing up to work five days a week, but whatever. A guy I consider the closest thing I got to a father just got grandpa-dumped in Bridgeport, Connecticut. And he's supposed to help me win this cockfight. No more money. No more help. All I want is a *fucking* recipe.
FLOYD. Who is gay?
ROSALIND. Nobody's, he's delusional —
WENDELL. Delusional? He shimmies up and down the Grand Concourse daily like a woman to the D train. *(To Floyd.)* I've been sick since you walked in this house. I don't even have the strength to tell my wife who's having a baby to stop smoking a cigarette in the bathroom. Try not to fuck anything up while I'm gone.
FLOYD. The park's closed.
WENDELL. Then I'm breaking in.

FLOYD. Ninety-five's got construction everywhere.

WENDELL. *Stop* lying to me. *(Smelling Lina's cigarette.)* Lina, stop smoking that fucking cigarette, that's my baby too! *(To Floyd.)* Give me the fucking keys.

FLOYD. Maybe you should ask Geronimo if it's okay. It's his car. *(Wendell grabs the keys and Felix's wallet from Floyd and exits.)*

ROSALIND. *(To Floyd.)* Well, at least you're getting along with your new family.

FLOYD. Who's gay? What the fuck was he talking about?

ROSALIND. Who the fuck knows.

FLOYD. What did he mean? Do you know what he's talking about?

ROSALIND. No.

FLOYD. You better not be lying to me.

ROSALIND. Oh no. I better not be lying to you. *(Beat. They regard each other.)*

FLOYD. You look good.

ROSALIND. So do you. *(Perhaps they make motion toward each other, to kiss, but this is interrupted when Lina enters from her bedroom with a handful of cash and crosses to Rosalind.)*

LINA. Here. Use this for your boys. We don't got enough to do anything worthwhile with it anyway. Like buy diapers. So why don't you have some? *(Lina hands Rosalind the cash.)*

ROSALIND. *Lina.*

FLOYD. My boys don't need anything.

LINA. Take it. It's the money you can't provide.

ROSALIND. Thanks Lina.

LINA. Now could you please leave?

ROSALIND. Sure.

LINA. Thank you. *(Rosalind heads towards the door.)*

ROSALIND. Just in case —

LINA. What? You get off welfare?

FLOYD. Jesus Lina. *(Rosalind exits, deeply hurt by this final insult. Pause.)* Lina. I apologize for crammin' my smells into your tiny apartment. This place is too small for three people.

LINA. It's like livin' with a whole lion shitting on the floor.

FLOYD. Yeah. I guess it is.

LINA. I can't believe you left your father at the track.

FLOYD. Try growing up with him, then without him, then with him, then you'll start to understand.

LINA. No, I don't think I would.

FLOYD. Well, I'm sorry about that.

LINA. You're a monster.

FLOYD. I know. I'm a monster.

LINA. He must be terrified.

FLOYD. Try being defenseless in a boy's home. That's also terrifying.

LINA. That excuse is so tired.

FLOYD. Bet it's not too tired a topic for Wendell.

LINA. Only *you* exploit your childhood for sympathy.

FLOYD. Maybe you should give Wendell some for his.

LINA. I do.

FLOYD. Do you have any idea what kinda woman his mother was? She was the kinda person who takes up five seats on the subway. Blubber and wheezing. She even had whiskers. You've seen the pictures. *(Beat.)* That said. If she hadn't a died. I woulda had nobody.

LINA. You gotta move out.

FLOYD. I will. Very very soon. *(Beat, then to the rooster.)* Well it looks like it's you and me, Calgary.

LINA. Calgary?

FLOYD. Yup. Calgary.

LINA. Calagay.

FLOYD. *Calagay? No.* Cal*gary*.

LINA. What?

FLOYD. This bird's from Canada. Wendell misheard. Geronimo can't speak. It's from Calgary, Canada. Not France.

LINA. *(Beat.)* I can't believe I'm gonna say this. It takes the romance out of it.

FLOYD. Tell me about it.

LINA. I think I'm still gonna call it Calagay.

FLOYD. I think that'll be fine. You should get into this rooster. It's a very handsome rooster.

LINA. I don't know if I can get into anything anymore.

FLOYD. No. Come here. Look at it. It looks good at night.

LINA. No. It's got like salmanilla. I'm gonna get bird flu.

FLOYD. No. Come look. *(Lina crosses to the bird.)*

LINA. It's so bright.

FLOYD. I know.

LINA. You did his feathers so nice.

FLOYD. I'm pretty good at that, yeah.

LINA. Your dad teach you that?

FLOYD. Yeah. *(Beat.)* Lina.

LINA. What?

FLOYD. Lina. I know you been drinking a lot lately. Even before you were pregnant. You should slow down.

LINA. The bird looks nice.

FLOYD. *(Beat.)* It does, doesn't it?

LINA. *(Gently.)* You know that note's not true, right?

FLOYD. Whatever's true, Lina, I'd like to not think about it. *(Pause.)*

LINA. *(Feeling something.)* Floyd, why you touchin' my leg.

FLOYD. Sorry. It was an accident.

LINA. No it wasn't.

FLOYD. OK.

LINA. That what you used to do? With the other ladies? Even after you were married?

FLOYD. No.

LINA. You'd sneak into their houses at night. When their husbands weren't home?

FLOYD. No.

LINA. That's what you did, wasn't it? And why Rosalind would always be crying over here. To Wendell.

FLOYD. She'd cry over here?

LINA. This is how you used to do it, right?

FLOYD. *(Beat.)* Yeah. Sometimes.

LINA. Floyd.

FLOYD. What.

LINA. Do it again. *(Beat.)* Hurry. *(Beat.)* 'Cause I got to get some sleep.

SCENE 7

Setting: Stadium-style seats at the greyhound track in Bridgeport, Connecticut. About an hour-and-a-half before dawn. At rise: Wendell sitting with Felix, who looks as though he has had a tough night. Felix is no longer sitting in the stadium seat, but instead squatting on the ground with the folding portion of the seat at his back.

WENDELL. So you just bunkered down here below your seat? So no one would see you?

FELIX. Yes. Yes. *(Stopping himself.)* They don't. Clean well, the management.

WENDELL. Obviously. Just write down the recipe. No more D-extract solvents. No more mean spirited notes. OK, Felix?

FELIX. I have. No pen.

WENDELL. I do. *(Handing a pen and paper to Felix.)* Ninety-five, the whole road, I hate this fucking state, write it down. *(Noticing the bottles at Felix's feet.)* Why do you got all these beer bottles you got at your feet.

FELIX. Floyd. Gave. Them. To me.

WENDELL. What kind of medication are you on?

FELIX. I. Am not. Sure.

WENDELL. How are you not sure?

FELIX. They just. Give. Them to me. *(Beat.)* Floyd-knows-though. He-talked-to-my. To my. *(Having trouble.)* Hot. Nurse.

WENDELL. Hot nurse?

FELIX. My hot nurse.

WENDELL. Damn. You look like hell. *(Looking around.)* How did they not see you here? I saw you right away.

FELIX. I was — lying-down. Long-ways. The seats. Looked normal. No one cleans. This dog track. *(Stopping himself, he reveals the Mexican short knife wrapped around his index finger as if it were a claw.)* I put this on. In case. Of attack.

WENDELL. What the fuck is that?

FELIX. Mexican. Short knife.

WENDELL. Mexican short knife? *(Felix nods.)* Where the fuck you get that? *(Felix shows Wendell the bag containing the dead bird, which has been practically torn open.)* What the fuck is that?

FELIX. Your. Dead rooster?

WENDELL. *(Knowing it is.)* Christ.

FELIX. It was here. When I woke. Up.

WENDELL. Your son must really hate you.

FELIX. Connecticut. Cockfighting. Cops. Bad.

WENDELL. Guess that's what you get for putting him in an orphanage.

FELIX. I have half. A body working. I cannot. Speak right. I am wearing. A Mexican short knife. At a dog track. I am paying. For mistakes. *(Pause.)*

WENDELL. She doesn't want to have my baby, Felix.

FELIX. Well. At least. You still. Have Michael.

WENDELL. You gotta stop it with that. I'm just trying to live my life.

FELIX. He's. *Good.* Michael.

WENDELL. Can't believe he visited you. By himself.

FELIX. Michael knows. He knows, I don't care. About gayness.

WENDELL. Write down the recipe. Don't fuck with me. Like you did Floyd.

FELIX. He-hit-me.

WENDELL. He saved me many times. Because he hit people. Somehow, if you look at it a certain way, you deserved this shit. Just write it down. I'm gonna sit here and not give you any food till you do. I got a burger in my pocket.

FELIX. He hit me. *Hard.*

WENDELL. *(Handing Felix a paper and pen.)* Just write it down. *(Felix begins to write.)* This better be a good fucking recipe.

FELIX. It. Is great.

WENDELL. You want to come to the cockfight with me?

FELIX. Where is it?

WENDELL. Washington Heights.

FELIX. No. Floyd hates me. He-will. Hit-me-again. Take me home.

WENDELL. Felix?

FELIX. Yeah.

WENDELL. When we take you home, you're gonna give me your second set of bird knives, okay? You're gonna do that for me.

FELIX. OK. *(Wendell takes the recipe from Felix.)*
WENDELL. *(Reading.)* This is the recipe?
FELIX. Yes.
WENDELL. *(Reading.)* Hartshorne?
FELIX. Get it. At the drug store. *(Handing Wendell the short knife.)* Here. Here is. Your short knife.
WENDELL. Thanks. *(Taking out the burger, biting into it, chewing.)* If it's all right. I think I'm gonna cry now. *(Wendell does not cry.)*

SCENE 8

Setting: The apartment. That morning. At rise: Geronimo preparing for today's match, going through various things, his old knives, solvents, perhaps he is even playing with the bird. Floyd, who has obviously been up all night, is staring right at him. The couch still has unmade bed sheets on it.

GERONIMO. Floyd.
FLOYD. What?
GERONIMO. Do not try and take my cash.
FLOYD. When?
GERONIMO. When we win. *(Holding out his hand.)* Shake.
FLOYD. On what?
GERONIMO. On that you will not take my money. *(Floyd shakes Geronimo's hand.)*
FLOYD. I won't take your money. *(Beat.)* It's a good thing you made me shake.
GERONIMO. Why?
FLOYD. 'Cause I'm disgusting. 'Cause I can't control myself.
GERONIMO. *(Sniffing.)* You smell funny.
FLOYD. Hey Geronimo.
GERONIMO. What?
FLOYD. Fuck you. *(Wendell enters with a carton of eggs and a stick of butter. He crosses to the stove to make eggs.)* We got a shitload to do, Wendell.
WENDELL. Well good, then you can feed them Felix's proper

recipe finally.

FLOYD. You got it?

WENDELL. Yeah, I got it. *And* I got the fuckin' knives. I got the knives and the recipe. You ready for this? It's fucking instant coffee, ground up Corn Flakes, and diced orange peels. How can you NOT remember this? It's made from basic household products. Like your childhood breakfast cereal. It's so easy to make it makes me want to punch you and Felix in the face.

FLOYD. Corn Flakes sounds familiar.

WENDELL. Of course it does.

FLOYD. *(Remembering.)* Corn Flakes?

WENDELL. Right, the oranges give the birds sugar, the coffee gives them caffeine, the combo makes them go bezerk.

FLOYD. Totally forgot about the cornflakes.

WENDELL. I guess that's why they put a rooster on the box. *(Beat.)* What you probably wouldn't have remembered. Was the hartshorne.

FLOYD. Hartshorne.

GERONIMO. *(Remembering.)* Hartshorne. He. That is right.

WENDELL. *(Sarcastic.)* What would we do without you, Nimo. *(To Floyd.)* It's like a medieval yeast. Or it's ground from deer antlers. I don't fuckin' know. Can't believe you can buy it in a drugstore. *(Beat.)* I'm so tired. Let's fucking make this thing.

FLOYD. Wendell. I gotta tell you something. 'Cause you're my good good friend. You always took care a me.

WENDELL. It's fine, man. It's what I do.

FLOYD. I fucked your wife. *(Long pause. Floyd stands and crosses to the kitchenette.)* Sit down. I'll make these eggs for you. *(Wendell sits down. Floyd lights the stove.)*

GERONIMO. What?

FLOYD. Geronimo, shut up. *(Floyd sprays Pam into a pan, then breaks three eggs into the skillet and lets them cook for a very short period of time, barely to a point in which they are solid.)*

GERONIMO. Floyd.

FLOYD. *Geronimo. (Floyd takes the barely cooked eggs, places them on a plate, sprinkles some salt and pepper on them, and places them in front of Wendell.)* I'm sorry. Here. I've made you some eggs.

WENDELL. Uh.

FLOYD. What.

WENDELL. Um.

44

FLOYD. What's the problem?

WENDELL. *(Referring to the eggs.)* They're really runny.

FLOYD. They cook while they sit there.

WENDELL. You have to put them back in the pan. 'Cause they're not cooked enough to even try to cook while they sit here.

FLOYD. They'll become eggs like you know them in a minute. Let them cook on your plate.

WENDELL. If you put them back in the pan I think they'll cook better.

FLOYD. Pops used to do it like this.

WENDELL. *(Beat, to Floyd.)* Why'd you sleep with my wife?

FLOYD. She's pregnant already. It can't happen twice. I think she's been with a lot of men, lately, Wendell. I could smell it on her. I didn't think it was fair, the way she was treating you. She's sleeping in the other room. Go talk to her.

WENDELL. She was treating me fine. *(Beat.)* These eggs are not cookin' while they sit here.

FLOYD. They will. Just hold out.

GERONIMO. I should leave. *(Wendell stands and crosses to the stove.)*

FLOYD. Rosalind's just a waste of your time, Wendell. She's just a waste of your time. *(With a growing rage, Wendell picks up the pan.)* And you know what? No wonder Michael's gotten so chubby since puberty.

WENDELL. *It's not my kid. (Perhaps in conjunction with the previous line, Wendell smashes the pan on Floyd's skull. Floyd falls down hard. To Floyd:)* Why can't a man just have a goddamn family for once? Why can't a man have a goddamn family?

SCENE 8A (optional)

Setting: The cockfight. That afternoon. At rise: spotlight up on Geronimo and Wendell with the rooster, presumably in the cockfighting ring. Wendell stands there reluctantly holding the cage as Geronimo removes the rooster from its pen, flaunts it about, blows in its beak, and gets it revved up for the fight. Wendell slowly pulls the cage from the ring in disbelief as Geronimo prepares to let the bird lose on its opponent.

SCENE 8B (optional)

Setting: The apartment. Early that evening. At rise: Rosalind enters and looks about at the tattered surroundings. She begins cleaning. By the time she is done, the apartment looks significantly more tidied than it did when she arrived.

SCENE 9

Setting: The apartment. Later that evening. At rise: Money stacked very high in several piles on the kitchen table, even more on the coffee tables and couch. Wendell is sitting at the table chewing on Wendy's chicken nuggets; an empty bag sits next to the meal. Geronimo stands in the bathroom, staring at the rooster, which is lying severely injured in the bathtub, out of view from the audience. It is barely breathing.

WENDELL. Jesus Christ.

GERONIMO. He is barely alive, but he is alive.

WENDELL. That's Calagay?

GERONIMO. Yes. That is him.

WENDELL. Oh man.

GERONIMO. We should keep him in the bath. He is still bleeding.

WENDELL. Sure. *(Referring to a gash he saw on the rooster's face.)* Did he lose an eye?

GERONIMO. Yeah. He did. The short knife has a very serious blade.

WENDELL. Nimo.

GERONIMO. What?

WENDELL. Should we just ... he's dying.

GERONIMO. No. If we can keep him alive we can breed him.

WENDELL. But. He's dying.

GERONIMO. But what if he does not.

WENDELL. This is one hell of a way to pay your bills.

GERONIMO. Where is my money?

WENDELL. *(Referring to the money.)* Your portion is over by the stove. *(Geronimo stops and stares at his portion.)*

GERONIMO. That is a *lot of fucking money.* Per volume.

WENDELL. It's organized in easy-to-deposit piles.

GERONIMO. I did not think it would be so ... so much.

WENDELL. Did you think it'd fit in your wallet?

GERONIMO. *Ay nako.* So much. *(Looking around the apartment, noticing it is cleaner.)* Who cleaned?

WENDELL. Rosalind came over. I think.

GERONIMO. Oh.

WENDELL. While we were at the fight. Lina's over there. Love to hear that conversation.

GERONIMO. I never handled birds before, in a ring like that. I didn't think I'd be ... good. When we lost the first fight. But man, after that. Three in a row. But when Calagay went down, I didn't get nervous, I stayed calm, just blew in his face, rubbed his beak. Then he destroyed that brown bird. *(Noticing the food-of-choice.)* Are you eating chicken?

WENDELL. Yes.

GERONIMO. Didn't you see the big bucket that said "Dead Roosters" pointing down?

WENDELL. That was gross. *(Beat.)* We won. *(Disbelief.)* Calagay made that brown chicken spit up blood.

GERONIMO. But he take it to the brain. Twice. He'll be okay.

WENDELL. That chicken. It winning? Was supposed to put my life back together, Nimo. Isn't that funny?

GERONIMO. In a short time, Floyd did a really good job conditioning these birds. What a talent. *(Beat.)* What are you going to do with Floyd's money?

WENDELL. Give it to him? That's what this whole thing was for, right? To get Floyd outta the house.

GERONIMO. *(Beat, then as delicately as possible.)* All of it? Wendell, he only had a hand in these birds for a little while.

WENDELL. *(Beat.)* What's that supposed to mean?

GERONIMO. I don't know.

WENDELL. I'd appreciate it if you wouldn't talk like that right now.

GERONIMO. Wendell.

WENDELL. What?

47

GERONIMO. He wasn't even at the fight.

WENDELL. So.

GERONIMO. We're the ones who won.

WENDELL. And he helped us train them.

GERONIMO. Yeah. And then he fucked your wife —

WENDELL. *Hey* —

GERONIMO. Yeah, what the fuck, give him his money —

WENDELL. *Woah* —

GERONIMO. Motherfucker fuck my wife I take a short knife to his throat.

WENDELL. Watch your fuckin' mouth Nimo —

GERONIMO. While you're at it why don't you take Lina back too, let everybody continue to eat the shit you made —

WENDELL. You better shut the fuck up.

GERONIMO. It's a lot of money Wendell —

WENDELL. *It belongs to people.*

GERONIMO. *Who?* Floyd? Rosalind? Lina? You behave like these people care for you.

WENDELL. You got no idea what you're talkin' about your wife's been dead so long. *(Pause.)* I'm sorry.

GERONIMO. *(Quietly, angrily, definitively.)* Do NOT underestimate grief.

WENDELL. I don't wanna go to a cockfight again.

GERONIMO. The way you behaved there, that makes sense.

WENDELL. I'm a fucking good man, Nimo. I'm a good person.

GERONIMO. Yeah, Wendell. That got you real far. *(Crossing back to the bathtub, then trying to will the rooster back to consciousness, lovingly, but with a sense of purpose.)* You're gonna make it bird.

SCENE 10

Setting: The apartment. About two weeks later. At rise: The place looks very different. Many of the piles have been either removed or placed against the wall. Lina, perhaps shaking a bit, looking very weak, is rocking the baby. The child is swaddled in pink. Wendell is unpacking groceries near the refrigerator.

LINA. *(To the child.)* Just sleep, honey. Just sleep.
WENDELL. She will.
LINA. Shh. She's getting there.
WENDELL. *(Beat.)* How are you feeling?
LINA. You need to stop asking me that.
WENDELL. I'll stop. Asking. *(Referring to the child.)* How's she doing?
LINA. She's very small.
WENDELL. *(Referring to the groceries.)* I got what you asked for.
LINA. Thanks.
WENDELL. You don't *have* to breast feed.
LINA. I'm breast feeding. I'm her mother.
WENDELL. You're low on energy.
LINA. I'm breast feeding.
WENDELL. *(Beat.)* OK.
LINA. Yeah.
WENDELL. Good. *(Beat.)* There's formula. It's powdered. It's in the cabinet. If you need it —
LINA. Pour it down the toilet.
WENDELL. It'll be in the cabinet. *(Wendell places the bag in the cabinet. Lina is oblivious to this.)* You want something to drink or something? Like a cola?
LINA. No.
WENDELL. I'm tired.
LINA. *(Looking about the place.)* Thanks for cleaning up. This place looks good. *(Wendell opens the refrigerator again. The entire unit is now filled with soft drinks. No alcohol is in sight. Wendell takes out a cola, opens it, takes a sip, then takes a cold burger from the refrig-*

erator and takes a bite.)

WENDELL. You guys look pretty calm. Sittin' there.

LINA. I don't feel that calm.

WENDELL. Well it's pretty calming. To look at the two of you.

LINA. At least somebody's calm.

WENDELL. You're like. We're like a big weird family. *(Lina admires the child, then looks at Wendell. After a moment, she actually smiles.)*

LINA. Do you think?

WENDELL. What?

LINA. We're like a big weird family?

WENDELL. Totally.

LINA. That's hilarious.

WENDELL. Why?

LINA. 'Cause this is one fucked up family.

WENDELL. It is, isn't it?

LINA. Totally. *(Referring to the baby.)* I just can't believe she is actually a real live baby. *(Wendell shoves the rest of the burger in his mouth and chews until he can speak.)*

WENDELL. Wish that shit was good for you. That tasted awesome.

LINA. *(Ruminating.)* A big weird family.

WENDELL. Totally. *(Wendell, smiling, takes a big sip from his cola, finishes the can, then throws it out.)* Lina. Did you never really love me? *(Long pause.)*

LINA. *(Meaning it.)* I love you. *(Beat. Wendell smiles. Lina smiles, then turns back around to admire the child. Then, without warning, Wendell falls over on the floor. Somehow, at first, Lina doesn't notice this, as if his fall was cushioned by a pillow. Beat.)* Wendell?

SCENE 11

Setting: Stadium-style seats at the greyhound track in Bridgeport, Connecticut. Two weeks later. At rise: Floyd holding a dog-racing ticket in his hand. Lina sits with him, holding the child.

FLOYD. We should stop by and give my dad some money, since we're here.

LINA. That. That is your call. *(Beat.)* I like your uniform.

FLOYD. Thanks. Nimo got new ones.

LINA. You look pretty handsome.

FLOYD. You know, everybody notices these things. It's weird. *(Beat.)* He just fell over?

LINA. Uh-huh. I barely heard him fall.

FLOYD. He's a big guy.

LINA. I've been through a lot, Floyd.

FLOYD. He wasn't exactly the type of guy who was gonna die of old age.

LINA. Floyd —

FLOYD. Massive heart attack was practically written on his birth certificate.

LINA. Please. Floyd. Not today.

FLOYD. *(Actually apologizing.)* OK. Sorry. Sometimes I can't stop myself.

LINA. I know. *(Beat.)* Thanks for taking me out of the house.

FLOYD. No problem.

LINA. This, this isn't exactly what I had in mind, the dog track, but thank you.

FLOYD. It's the only place I know. That I feel calm.

LINA. Well I'd say that's a pretty weird phenomenon. *(The starting bell is heard.)*

FLOYD. *(Looking.)* They come around the track fast.

LINA. *(Looking.)* They're so skinny.

FLOYD. *(Flashing his ticket in the air.)* C'mon FIVE, you mother-fucker.

LINA. It's bad enough we're sitting with her at the dog track. Please don't curse.

FLOYD. *(Referring to the racing dogs again.)* Five is totally gonna shit the bed.

LINA. Floyd.

FLOYD. OK. Last curse. Swear.

LINA. *(Noticing his dog is losing.)* You're a bad gambler.

FLOYD. I just guessed wrong.

LINA. You can raise a rooster, but you're a bad gambler.

FLOYD. Well I'll try to do better with our champion rooster babies. I won everybody a lot of money, Lina.

LINA. I know.

FLOYD. I'd appreciate a thank you once in a while.

51

LINA. Thank you.

FLOYD. *(Beat.)* Just wait till these birds hit again.

LINA. Floyd. If it's okay. No more birds. For me.

FLOYD. *(Hurt?)* OK. *(Beat.)* What if. The kid needs help?

LINA. Floyd. She's not your kid.

FLOYD. *(Beat.)* If you try and be nice then I'll continue to try and be nice too.

LINA. OK. *(Beat.)* If you want to focus on a kid, focus on Theo. He's a nice kid.

FLOYD. *(Beat.)* You think so?

LINA. And Michael. For what it's worth. He's … upstanding. You should be proud.

FLOYD. I am. Of both of them.

LINA. *(Beat.)* Best if you not tell Rosalind about the money.

FLOYD. I think she'd understand, Rosalind, if I told her.

LINA. I don't think so.

FLOYD. *(Beat, the referring to Wendell.)* I'm going to really really miss him.

LINA. Me too.

FLOYD. *(Pause, referring to the child.)* It's kind of weird. That he's inside of that, huh? *(Lina cannot really contain her sadness at this idea. She turns away to not let Floyd see her upset.)* Lina?

LINA. What?

FLOYD. When you gonna name the baby?

LINA. What?

FLOYD. She should have a name. It's been a long time.

LINA. I can't decide. With Wendell and everything.

FLOYD. I just call her baby. It's kind of demented. *(Beat.)* You gotta name her.

LINA. What?

FLOYD. What?

LINA. What do I name her?

FLOYD. I don't know. You're the mom.

LINA. I don't know what to name her.

FLOYD. Name her after your mother, I don't know.

LINA. Are you kidding me?

FLOYD. This is sick, Lina. The child should have a name.

LINA. You name her.

FLOYD. It's not my baby.

LINA. You should help me name her something.

FLOYD. Oh no, don't do that to me.

LINA. Well then she won't have a name for a little longer. Watch your race.

FLOYD. It's over. I lost.

LINA. Then wait for the next one. *(Beat.)* Pass me the bottle.

FLOYD. *(Doing so.)* Thought you were breast feeding.

LINA. I am. It's in the bottle.

FLOYD. You can do that?

LINA. For several decades now we've been able to do this.

FLOYD. Oh. *(Floyd watches Lina feed the child. Beat.)* How about Isabelle?

LINA. What?

FLOYD. Is Isabelle a nice name?

LINA. *(Considering.)* Why Isabelle?

FLOYD. 'Cause she is …

LINA. What?

FLOYD. 'Cause she … *is a bell.*

LINA. *(Considering some more.)* Isabelle.

FLOYD. Or something. I don't know. Name the fucking human being.

LINA. Isabelle.

FLOYD. That's the only girl name in my arsenal.

LINA. Isabelle.

FLOYD. Run it by the girls at Macy's. Take a vote.

LINA. Isabelle.

FLOYD. I don't want to be responsible for this. Decide for your-self. I'm simply an advisor. *(Looking at the child.)* She is pretty cute, though. If little.

LINA. She's like, a little unit of a human.

FLOYD. *(Tearing?)* Please stop. *(Beat.)* If you ever need anything, Lina. Like to get out of the house, like we've done today. Just know you can come to me. Just know that. I'll try and keep this job for as long I can. Rosalind will just have to understand.

LINA. Thanks Floyd. But I'm fine. *(Then, regarding Wendell? Regarding leaving the park?)* What are we gonna do?

FLOYD. I don't know. *(Beat.)* I'd just like to sit for a second. Before we go.

LINA. We're going?

FLOYD. Yeah. I'd just like to sit for a second, though.

LINA. OK.

FLOYD. In quiet. I'd just like to sit quiet for a second. In quiet. *(They sit in quiet for about ten seconds.)*

End of Play

PROPERTY LIST

Rooster in cage
Piles of papers: coupons, envelopes, etc.
Varieties of fast food bags (McDonald's, Wendy's, etc.) with food
Shopping bags
Pack of cigarettes
Jar of pickles
Slip of paper with recipe
Medical tubing
Brown lunch bags
Bowl
Mexican short knife
Car keys
Television set
Mail
Various cans of beer and soda
Dog-racing magazine
Pad and pen
Six pack beer
Sipping straw
Two wallets with cash, ID's, photos, etc.
Cigarette lighter
Kitchen garbage can
Two hamburgers on a plate
Cash on hand
Various knives
Equipment for cockfighting
Carton of eggs
Stick of butter
Pam spray
Fry pan
Plate
Salt and pepper
Piles of money
Swaddled "baby"
Housecleaning supplies
Dog-racing ticket

SOUND EFFECTS

Keys opening door
TV talk show
Starting bell at dog race
Knocks at door

Set design by Victoria Imperioli

A rendering of the set design for the Studio Dante production of *Chicken*.

Painting by Mark Turgeon

NEW PLAYS

★ **GUARDIANS by Peter Morris.** In this unflinching look at war, a disgraced American soldier discloses the truth about Abu Ghraib prison, and a clever English journalist reveals how he faked a similar story for the London tabloids. "Compelling, sympathetic and powerful." *–NY Times.* "Sends you into a state of moral turbulence." *–Sunday Times (UK).* "Nothing short of remarkable." *–Village Voice.* [1M, 1W] ISBN: 978-0-8222-2177-7

★ **BLUE DOOR by Tanya Barfield.** Three generations of men (all played by one actor), from slavery through Black Power, challenge Lewis, a tenured professor of mathematics, to embark on a journey combining past and present. "A teasing flare for words." *–Village Voice.* "Unfailingly thought-provoking." *–LA Times.* "The play moves with the speed and logic of a dream." *–Seattle Weekly.* [2M] ISBN: 978-0-8222-2209-5

★ **THE INTELLIGENT DESIGN OF JENNY CHOW by Rolin Jones.** This irreverent "techno-comedy" chronicles one brilliant woman's quest to determine her heritage and face her fears with the help of her astounding creation called Jenny Chow. "Boldly imagined." *–NY Times.* "Fantastical and funny." *–Variety.* "Harvests many laughs and finally a few tears." *–LA Times.* [3M, 3W] ISBN: 978-0-8222-2071-8

★ **SOUVENIR by Stephen Temperley.** Florence Foster Jenkins, a wealthy society eccentric, suffers under the delusion that she is a great coloratura soprano—when in fact the opposite is true. "Hilarious and deeply touching. Incredibly moving and breathtaking." *–NY Daily News.* "A sweet love letter of a play." *–NY Times.* "Wildly funny. Completely charming." *–Star-Ledger.* [1M, 1W] ISBN: 978-0-8222-2157-9

★ **ICE GLEN by Joan Ackermann.** In this touching period comedy, a beautiful poetess dwells in idyllic obscurity on a Berkshire estate with a band of unlikely cohorts. "A beautifully written story of nature and change." *–Talkin' Broadway.* "A lovely play which will leave you with a lot to think about." *–CurtainUp.* "Funny, moving and witty." *–Metroland (Boston).* [4M, 3W] ISBN: 978-0-8222-2175-3

★ **THE LAST DAYS OF JUDAS ISCARIOT by Stephen Adly Guirgis.** Set in a time-bending, darkly comic world between heaven and hell, this play reexamines the plight and fate of the New Testament's most infamous sinner. "An unforced eloquence that finds the poetry in lowdown street talk." *–NY Times.* "A real jaw-dropper." *–Variety.* "An extraordinary play." *–Guardian (UK).* [10M, 5W] ISBN: 978-0-8222-2082-4

DRAMATISTS PLAY SERVICE, INC.
440 Park Avenue South, New York, NY 10016 212-683-8960 Fax 212-213-1539
postmaster@dramatists.com www.dramatists.com

NEW PLAYS

★ **THE GREAT AMERICAN TRAILER PARK MUSICAL music and lyrics by David Nehls, book by Betsy Kelso.** Pippi, a stripper on the run, has just moved into Armadillo Acres, wreaking havoc among the tenants of Florida's most exclusive trailer park. "Adultery, strippers, murderous ex-boyfriends, Costco and the Ice Capades. Undeniable fun." *–NY Post.* "Joyful and unashamedly vulgar." *–The New Yorker.* "Sparkles with treasure." *–New York Sun.* [2M, 5W] ISBN: 978-0-8222-2137-1

★ **MATCH by Stephen Belber.** When a young Seattle couple meet a prominent New York choreographer, they are led on a fraught journey that will change their lives forever. "Uproariously funny, deeply moving, enthralling theatre." *–NY Daily News.* "Prolific laughs and ear-to-ear smiles." *–NY Magazine.* [2M, 1W] ISBN: 978-0-8222-2020-6

★ **MR. MARMALADE by Noah Haidle.** Four-year-old Lucy's imaginary friend, Mr. Marmalade, doesn't have much time for her—not to mention he has a cocaine addiction and a penchant for pornography. "Alternately hilarious and heartbreaking." *–The New Yorker.* "A mature and accomplished play." *–LA Times.* "Scathingly observant comedy." *–Miami Herald.* [4M, 2W] ISBN: 978-0-8222-2142-5

★ **MOONLIGHT AND MAGNOLIAS by Ron Hutchinson.** Three men cloister themselves as they work tirelessly to reshape a screenplay that's just not working—*Gone with the Wind.* "Consumers of vintage Hollywood insider stories will eat up Hutchinson's diverting conjecture." *–Variety.* "A lot of fun." *–NY Post.* "A Hollywood dream-factory farce." *–Chicago Sun-Times.* [3M, 1W] ISBN: 978-0-8222-2084-8

★ **THE LEARNED LADIES OF PARK AVENUE by David Grimm, translated and freely adapted from Molière's *Les Femmes Savantes*.** Dicky wants to marry Betty, but her mother's plan is for Betty to wed a most pompous man. "A brave, brainy and barmy revision." *–Hartford Courant.* "A rare but welcome bird in contemporary theatre." *–New Haven Register.* "Roll over Cole Porter." *–Boston Globe.* [5M, 5W] ISBN: 978-0-8222-2135-7

★ **REGRETS ONLY by Paul Rudnick.** A sparkling comedy of Manhattan manners that explores the latest topics in marriage, friendships and squandered riches. "One of the funniest quip-meisters on the planet." *–NY Times.* "Precious moments of hilarity. Devastatingly accurate political and social satire." *–BackStage.* "Great fun." *–CurtainUp.* [3M, 3W] ISBN: 978-0-8222-2223-1

DRAMATISTS PLAY SERVICE, INC.
440 Park Avenue South, New York, NY 10016 212-683-8960 Fax 212-213-1539
postmaster@dramatists.com www.dramatists.com

NEW PLAYS

★ **AFTER ASHLEY by Gina Gionfriddo.** A teenager is unwillingly thrust into the national spotlight when a family tragedy becomes talk-show fodder. "A work that virtually any audience would find accessible." –*NY Times.* "Deft characterization and caustic humor." –*NY Sun.* "A smart satirical drama." –*Variety.* [4M, 2W] ISBN: 978-0-8222-2099-2

★ **THE RUBY SUNRISE by Rinne Groff.** Twenty-five years after Ruby struggles to realize her dream of inventing the first television, her daughter faces similar battles of faith as she works to get Ruby's story told on network TV. "Measured and intelligent, optimistic yet clear-eyed." –*NY Magazine.* "Maintains an exciting sense of ingenuity." –*Village Voice.* "Sinuous theatrical flair." –*Broadway.com.* [3M, 4W] ISBN: 978-0-8222-2140-1

★ **MY NAME IS RACHEL CORRIE taken from the writings of Rachel Corrie, edited by Alan Rickman and Katharine Viner.** This solo piece tells the story of Rachel Corrie who was killed in Gaza by an Israeli bulldozer set to demolish a Palestinian home. "Heartbreaking urgency. An invigoratingly detailed portrait of a passionate idealist." –*NY Times.* "Deeply authentically human." –*USA Today.* "A stunning dramatization." –*CurtainUp.* [1W] ISBN: 978-0-8222-2222-4

★ **ALMOST, MAINE by John Cariani.** This charming midwinter night's dream of a play turns romantic clichés on their ear as it chronicles the painfully hilarious amorous adventures (and misadventures) of residents of a remote northern town that doesn't quite exist. "A whimsical approach to the joys and perils of romance." –*NY Times.* "Sweet, poignant and witty." –*NY Daily News.* "Aims for the heart by way of the funny bone." –*Star-Ledger.* [2M, 2W] ISBN: 978-0-8222-2156-2

★ **Mitch Albom's TUESDAYS WITH MORRIE by Jeffrey Hatcher and Mitch Albom, based on the book by Mitch Albom.** The true story of Brandeis University professor Morrie Schwartz and his relationship with his student Mitch Albom. "A touching, life-affirming, deeply emotional drama." –*NY Daily News.* "You'll laugh. You'll cry." –*Variety.* "Moving and powerful." –*NY Post.* [2M] ISBN: 978-0-8222-2188-3

★ **DOG SEES GOD: CONFESSIONS OF A TEENAGE BLOCKHEAD by Bert V. Royal.** An abused pianist and a pyromaniac ex-girlfriend contribute to the teen-angst of America's most hapless kid. "A welcome antidote to the notion that the *Peanuts* gang provides merely American cuteness." –*NY Times.* "Hysterically funny." –*NY Post.* "The *Peanuts* kids have finally come out of their shells." –*Time Out.* [4M, 4W] ISBN: 978-0-8222-2152-4

DRAMATISTS PLAY SERVICE, INC.
440 Park Avenue South, New York, NY 10016 212-683-8960 Fax 212-213-1539
postmaster@dramatists.com *www.dramatists.com*

NEW PLAYS

★ **RABBIT HOLE by David Lindsay-Abaire.** Winner of the 2007 Pulitzer Prize. Becca and Howie Corbett have everything a couple could want until a life-shattering accident turns their world upside down. "An intensely emotional examination of grief, laced with wit." *–Variety.* "A transcendent and deeply affecting new play." *–Entertainment Weekly.* "Painstakingly beautiful." *–BackStage.* [2M, 3W] ISBN: 978-0-8222-2154-8

★ **DOUBT, A Parable by John Patrick Shanley.** Winner of the 2005 Pulitzer Prize and Tony Award. Sister Aloysius, a Bronx school principal, takes matters into her own hands when she suspects the young Father Flynn of improper relations with one of the male students. "All the elements come invigoratingly together like clockwork." *–Variety.* "Passionate, exquisite, important, engrossing." *–NY Newsday.* [1M, 3W] ISBN: 978-0-8222-2219-4

★ **THE PILLOWMAN by Martin McDonagh.** In an unnamed totalitarian state, an author of horrific children's stories discovers that someone has been making his stories come true. "A blindingly bright black comedy." *–NY Times.* "McDonagh's least forgiving, bravest play." *–Variety.* "Thoroughly startling and genuinely intimidating." *–Chicago Tribune.* [4M, 5 bit parts (2M, 1W, 1 boy, 1 girl)] ISBN: 978-0-8222-2100-5

★ **GREY GARDENS book by Doug Wright, music by Scott Frankel, lyrics by Michael Korie.** The hilarious and heartbreaking story of Big Edie and Little Edie Bouvier Beale, the eccentric aunt and cousin of Jacqueline Kennedy Onassis, once bright names on the social register who became East Hampton's most notorious recluses. "An experience no passionate theatergoer should miss." *–NY Times.* "A unique and unmissable musical." *–Rolling Stone.* [4M, 3W, 2 girls] ISBN: 978-0-8222-2181-4

★ **THE LITTLE DOG LAUGHED by Douglas Carter Beane.** Mitchell Green could make it big as the hot new leading man in Hollywood if Diane, his agent, could just keep him in the closet. "Devastatingly funny." *–NY Times.* "An out-and-out delight." *–NY Daily News.* "Full of wit and wisdom." *–NY Post.* [2M, 2W] ISBN: 978-0-8222-2226-2

★ **SHINING CITY by Conor McPherson.** A guilt-ridden man reaches out to a therapist after seeing the ghost of his recently deceased wife. "Haunting, inspired and glorious." *–NY Times.* "Simply breathtaking and astonishing." *–Time Out.* "A thoughtful, artful, absorbing new drama." *–Star-Ledger.* [3M, 1W] ISBN: 978-0-8222-2187-6

DRAMATISTS PLAY SERVICE, INC.
440 Park Avenue South, New York, NY 10016 212-683-8960 Fax 212-213-1539
postmaster@dramatists.com www.dramatists.com